The Value of Self Care

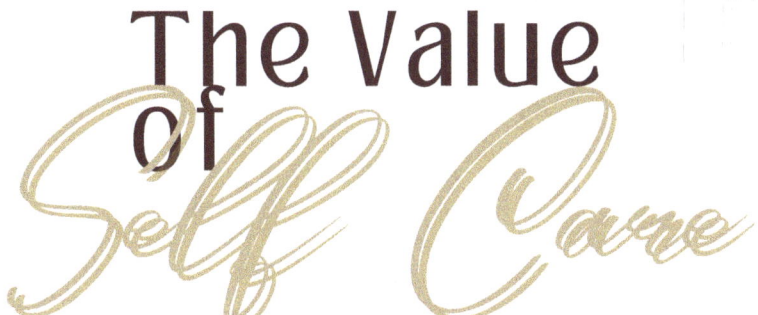

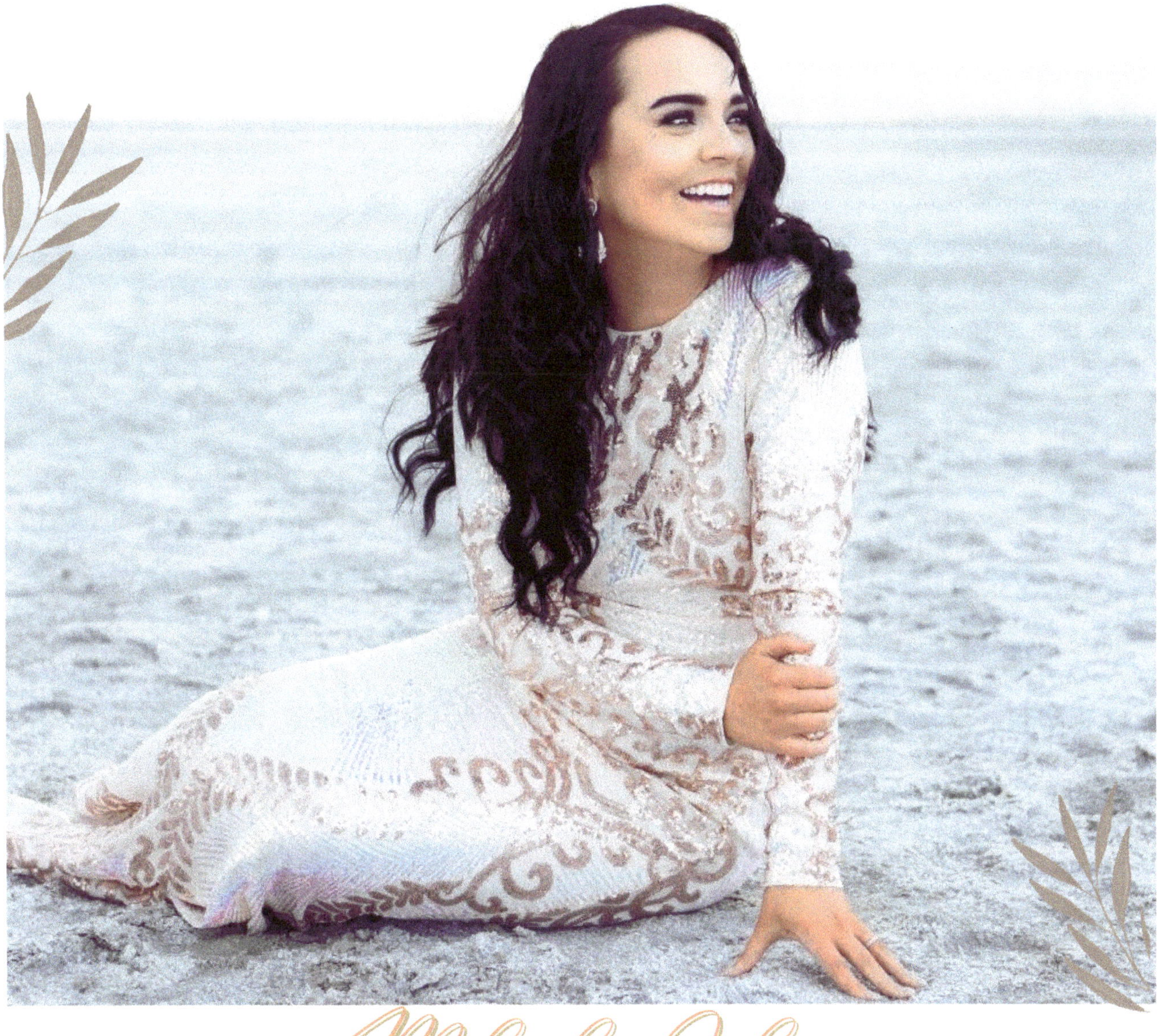

Mckayla Julian

A guided self-care workbook

Introducing
MCKAYLA JULIAN

As the founder of Pretty Tough Ladies, I am honored you have chosen this workbook to guide you on your self-care and healing journey.

Pretty Tough Ladies is a center that provides resources and essential items to women and children who are escaping domestic violence and in trauma recovery. My personal journey of overcoming domestic violence began in 2020 after leaving my abuser. I founded Pretty Tough Ladies in April 2022, and in May 2022, decided to take my healing to the next level and invest in myself with in-depth trauma therapy and sobriety.

During the following years, Pretty Tough Ladies has been honored to serve over 6,000 women and children on their own healing journey. Through the process, I have learned, healed, and grown in more ways than I thought possible, and am eager to share this growth and knowledge with you because I know you'll do great things with it.

You are capable.
You are worthy.
You are loved.

Much love,

Mckayla Julian

TABLE OF CONTENTS

 Make Self-Care a Priority

 Identify Your Needs

 Create Self-Care Routine

 Practice Self-Compassion

 Set Boundaries

 Get Enough Rest

 Connect with Others

 Take Care of Your Phsical Self

LIMITING BELIEFS

Before we discuss self-care and its importance, let's discuss "Limiting Beliefs."

Each of us carries within ourselves a unique set of beliefs, ideas, and convictions that shape how we perceive the world and, more importantly, ourselves. Sometimes, these beliefs can become shackles that hold us back from realizing our full potential and living our desired life.

Limiting beliefs are negative and self-defeating thoughts that convince us we are not capable, worthy, or deserving of success, happiness, or fulfillment. They often manifest as inner voices that tell us we're not good, smart, or talented enough. These beliefs can be deeply ingrained and developed through years of conditioning and experiences. However, these beliefs are not truths but rather distortions of our capabilities.

The first step in overcoming limiting beliefs is to recognize and acknowledge them. It is crucial to understand that these beliefs are not facts but interpretations of our past experiences and societal conditioning. They result from fear, self-doubt, and the influence of others who may have projected their own limitations onto us. When we expose these beliefs and bring them into our conscious awareness, we can begin to challenge their validity.

Once we've identified these limiting beliefs, we can start reframing them by replacing them with empowering and positive beliefs that reflect our true potential. Instead of saying, "I'm not good enough," we can affirm, "I am constantly growing and improving."

Rather than believing, "I can't do it," we can declare, "I am capable, and I will find a way." This shift in perspective is a powerful tool for breaking free from self-doubt.

Seeking inspiration and guidance from those who have overcome similar challenges can be invaluable. Countless stories of individuals defied the odds, shattered their limiting beliefs, and achieved extraordinary success. These stories serve as beacons of hope and proof that our potential is limitless when we dare to challenge our negative thinking.

Another essential aspect of overcoming limiting beliefs is self-compassion. We must learn to treat ourselves with kindness and patience as we embark on this transformative journey. We will encounter setbacks and moments of self-doubt along the way, but these are not failures but opportunities for growth and learning. By nurturing self-compassion, we can weather these storms and keep moving forward.

Taking action is critical to breaking the grip of limiting beliefs. It's not enough to change our thoughts; we must also change our behaviors. By setting achievable goals, stepping out of our comfort zones, and celebrating small victories, we prove to ourselves that we are capable of more than we once believed.

Limiting beliefs may be deeply rooted, but they are not insurmountable. We have the power within us to challenge and overcome these beliefs that hold us back from realizing our full potential.

By recognizing, reframing, seeking inspiration, practicing self-compassion, and taking action, we can break free from the chains of self-doubt and unlock the doors to a future filled with success, happiness, and fulfillment.

5-Step Process

 **CHOOSE** a topic you want to clear limiting beliefs on.

 **WRITE** a list of limiting beliefs you have around this topic.

 **THANK** these beliefs for how they have protected you.

 **FORGIVE** yourself and others for these beliefs you have developed.

 **GIVE** yourself permission to honor these beliefs and move past them.

List the most Prominent Limiting Beliefs Holding You Back:

SELF:

_____
_____
_____
_____
_____
_____
_____

SUCCESS:

_____
_____
_____
_____
_____
_____
_____

LOVE:

_____
_____
_____
_____
_____
_____
_____

MONEY:

_____
_____
_____
_____
_____
_____
_____

UNIT ONE

MAKE SELF-CARE A PRIORITY

REDUCED STRESS

In the hustle and bustle of our lives, it's easy to forget that we are our most important asset.

Self-care is not a luxury; it's a necessity. It's about recognizing our worth and nurturing our physical, emotional, and mental well-being. Self-care enables us to be our best selves, show up for our loved ones, and tackle life's challenges with resilience and strength. It's the foundation for a healthier, happier, and more fulfilling life.

Self-care is about setting boundaries, learning to say 'No' when necessary, and permitting ourselves to rest, recharge, and find moments of joy. It's about choosing healthier options for our bodies, seeking help when needed, and addressing our emotional needs.

If we don't take care of ourselves, we risk burnout, physical and mental health issues, and the erosion of our happiness. Neglecting self-care harms us and affects our ability to effectively care for others.

So, let us consciously put ourselves first, not out of vanity, but out of self-respect, love, and necessity. Commit to self-care, recognizing that it is not a one-time act but a lifelong practice. In doing so, we empower ourselves to live our lives to the fullest and positively influence those around us.

Remember, you are worth the time and effort required for self-care. By making it a priority, you will enhance your life and become a beacon of inspiration for others.

Take care of yourself because you are the most important project you will ever work on.

You are MORE than

Enough

Self-Care Strategies

It's harder to plan when you're overwhelmed or in a crisis.

However, planning for challenges before they happen gives you insight into the best and most sustainable options to recharge and recharge your batteries.

Also, each day, proactively taking care of yourself in small ways helps you be better prepared for challenges or unforeseen circumstances.

THINGS I CAN DO EACH DAY THAT WILL MAKE ME FEEL GOOD ABOUT MYSELF

WHAT I SHOULD SAY TO MYSELF WHEN I AM HAVING A DIFFICULT TIME:

WHAT I SHOULD AVOID DOING WHEN I AM HAVING A HARD DAY

WHAT I CAN DO (THAT IS GOOD FOR ME) WHEN I FEEL OVERWHELMED OR UPSET

Self-Care Quiz

There are no right or wrong answers; simply respond as you see fit and see what you discover about yourself.

Score 2 points for each 'Yes',

1 point for each 'S / Sometimes'

0 point for 'No'.

		Yes	S	No
1.	I am up-to-date with my health check-ups	☐	☐	☐
2.	I am happy with my physical fitness	☐	☐	☐
3.	I eat well nutritionally most of the time	☐	☐	☐
4.	I have plenty of sleep and feel well-rested	☐	☐	☐
5.	I take regular breaks from my work	☐	☐	☐
6.	I say "No" to others when I need to	☐	☐	☐
7.	I have forgiven my past mistakes	☐	☐	☐
8.	I know what I am passionate about	☐	☐	☐
9.	I have things to look forward to in my life	☐	☐	☐

Your total score _____

What did you learn about yourself?

Self-Care Plan

GOALS FOR MY MIND

▶

▷

▷

▶

GOALS FOR MY BODY

▶

▷

▷

▶

GOOD RULES & HABITS I WANT TO LIVE BY:

- ## MIND

  ### Mental health

  Mindfulness and self knowledge

  ### Soul

  Stimulation and fulfillment

- ## BODY

  ### Self-care

  Basic hygiene and body care

  ### Improvement

  Exercise, sleep and healthy food

Self-Care

Making the Most of Every Self Care Practice

Score tasks based firstly on their impact and secondly on the effort needed to complete them.

(0 for no real effort or impact to 10 for a major effort or impact).

Self Care Activity	Impact (0-10)	Effort (0-10)

Vision Board

HEALTH

LOVE

FAMILY

CAREER

Self-Awareness Assessment

READ THE PROMTS BELOW AND THINK ABOUT THE FIRST THING THAT COMES TO MIND. FILL YOUR ANSWERS OUT IN THE BLANK BOXES.

I AM A HUMAN BEING THAT...

LOVES	
WANTS TO	
IS DRIVEN BY	
IS INSPIRED BY	
HAS A HABIT OF	
IS HAPPIEST WHEN	
BELIEVES IN	
WOULD GIVE	
WILL ONE DAY	
HAS THE GOAL OF	
WHO NOTICES	
IS AFRAID OF	

INCREASED RESILIENCE

Let us begin by understanding what self-care truly means. It is not merely indulging in occasional spa days or vacations, although those can be part of it.

Self-care encompasses a holistic approach to nurturing physical, emotional, and mental well-being. It involves setting aside time for self-reflection, relaxation, and self-improvement. It means prioritizing ourselves, not out of selfishness, but out of the recognition that we cannot pour from an empty cup.

Now, let's explore the profound connection between self-care and resilience.

Resilience is our ability to bounce back from setbacks, adapt to change, and thrive despite adversity. It is not a quality we are born with but rather a skill that can be cultivated.

Self-care is the soil from which resilience can grow and allows us to recharge. Like a battery, we, too, have limits to our energy and emotional reserves.

Neglecting self-care can lead to burnout, leaving us emotionally and physically depleted. When we consistently practice self-care, we replenish our reserves, giving us the strength to withstand life's challenges.

Self-care empowers us with self-awareness.

When we take the time to reflect on our thoughts and emotions, we become better equipped to understand our reactions to stressors. This self-awareness enables us to develop healthier coping mechanisms and problem-solving skills, enhancing our ability to bounce back from adversity.

Self-care nurtures our mental and emotional health.

Engaging in activities that bring us joy, like hobbies or spending quality time with loved ones, releases endorphins and reduces stress hormones. These positive experiences boost our mood and fortify our emotional well-being, making us more resilient to life's ups and downs.

Self-care fosters a sense of self-compassion.

When we treat ourselves with kindness and prioritize our own well-being, we develop a more compassionate attitude. This self-compassion becomes a powerful ally during challenging times, helping us bounce back from setbacks without self-judgment or criticism.

Self-care builds a strong foundation for effective problem-solving.

When rested, emotionally balanced, and mentally clear, we are better equipped to assess situations rationally and make informed decisions. This critical component of resilience enables us to confront adversity with a clear mind and a proactive attitude.

Assessing Yourself

Physical Self Care Mental Self Care

Physical Self Care

	Y	N
Got Enough Sleep	○	○
Eat healthy	○	○
Balanced Diet	○	○
Get Regular Exercise See	○	○
a Healthcare	○	○
Provider when needed	○	○

NOTE:

Mental Self Care

	Y	N
Take time to relax	○	○
Joy and Fulfillment in activities	○	○
Support System	○	○
Practice Mindfullness	○	○
Stay present in the moment	○	○

NOTE:

Social Self Care

	Y	N
Strong and Supportive Relationship with friends and family	○	○
Make time for social activity	○	○
Set Boundaries	○	○
Say no when necessary	○	○

NOTE:

Spiritual Self Care

	Y	N
Have a sense of purpose and meaning in your life	○	○
Practice self-reflection and mindfulness	○	○
Have a sense of connection to something larger than yourself	○	○

NOTE:

Questions to Myself

Are my goals really
what I want?

Answer in one word: What is
between me and the dream
life/my main goal?

Ask what does the
word "happiness"
mean to me?

Do I drive conscious or
mass consumption?

What disadvantages of
another person am I not
willing to put up with?

How could I simplify my
life and focus on what
is most important?

BETTER MENTAL HEALTH

Our mental health is the cornerstone of our overall well-being. It affects how we think, feel, and act and influences every aspect of our lives.

Yet, amid our daily responsibilities and challenges, we often overlook the importance of nurturing our mental health.

Self-care, in its many forms, is the answer to this oversight. It encompasses many practices and activities that promote our mental and emotional well-being. Whether practicing mindfulness, engaging in creative pursuits, seeking therapy, or simply taking time for relaxation and self-reflection, self-care is necessary to build and maintain a healthy mind.

One of the most significant benefits of self-care is its capacity to reduce stress and anxiety. In our fast-paced lives, stress is an ever-present companion, and chronic stress can take a toll on our mental health.

Self-care provides us with the tools to manage and alleviate stress, allowing us to regain control and inner peace. Activities such as meditation and deep breathing exercises help calm our nervous systems, reducing the production of stress hormones like cortisol. Engaging in these practices regularly can lead to improved emotional resilience, making us better equipped to face life's challenges with a clear mind and a steady heart.

Self-care also fosters self-compassion, a crucial component of good mental health. When we engage in self-care, we send a powerful message to ourselves—that we are worthy of love, care, and attention.

This self-compassion helps counteract negative self-talk and self-criticism, which can contribute to conditions like depression and anxiety.

Self-care promotes emotional self-regulation. It teaches us to identify and manage our emotions healthily, reducing the risk of emotional volatility and mood disorders.

By incorporating self-care into our lives, we can respond to challenging situations with greater emotional intelligence and resilience.

Self-care creates opportunities for self-reflection and personal growth. When we take time for ourselves, we can explore our thoughts, feelings, and goals more deeply. This self-awareness is essential for identifying and addressing any mental health challenges we may face, as well as for setting and pursuing personal and professional aspirations.

Gratitude Tracker

1. _____
2. _____
3. _____
4. _____
5. _____
6. _____
7. _____
8. _____
9. _____
10. _____
11. _____
12. _____
13. _____
14. _____
15. _____
16.

17. _____
18. _____
19. _____
20. _____
21. _____
22. _____
23. _____
24. _____
25. _____
26. _____
27. _____
28. _____
29. _____
30. _____
31. _____

Setting Goals and Prioritizing Self-Care

Your Goals :

Priority Goals:

Self-Care Checklist

- Drink a glass of water to start the day

- Enjoy 15-30 minutes of exercise

- Get some fresh air

- Have a healthy breakfast

- Enjoy a warm morning drink

- Plan out your day in your planner

- Stretch your body

- Take regular breaks

- Enjoy some sunshine

- Take hot/Cold bath or shower

- Read something meaningful

- Play some invigorating music

- Disconnect

- Eat a healthy snack

- Wind down by avoiding bright light at night Get in bed before 10pm

UNIT TWO

IDENTIFY YOUR NEEDS

Identifying your self-care needs is an important step in making self-care a priority in your life.

Here are some exercises to help you identify your self-care needs:

Self-Reflection:
Reflect on your life and identify areas where you feel stressed, overwhelmed, or unfulfilled. Think about past activities or practices that have helped you feel better, and consider incorporating them into your self-care routine.

Body Scan:
Take a few minutes to do a body scan, paying attention to any physical sensations of discomfort or tension. Consider activities that may help alleviate these feelings, such as stretching, exercise, or massage.

Emotional Check-In:
Check in with your emotions and identify any patterns of stress or anxiety. Consider activities that help you manage these emotions, such as journaling, talking to a friend, or practicing mindfulness.

Lifestyle Assessment:
Evaluate your daily habits and routines, and consider ways to incorporate self-care practices into your daily life. For example, you may prioritize sleep, eat a healthier diet, or schedule time for exercise or hobbies.

Strengths Assessment:
Identify your strengths and consider ways to use them to promote self-care. If you are creative, you may find joy in painting or writing, which can be incorporated into your self-care routine.

Remember, each individual's self-care needs are unique, and it's important to explore what works best for you. By identifying your needs, you can develop a self-care routine that promotes physical, emotional, and mental well-being.

As you are building your self- care plan, the following steps can be helpful:

Assess your needs:

Make a list of the different parts of your life and significant activities that you engage in each day. Some of you might list work, school, relationships, and family.

Consider your stressors:

Think about the aspects of these areas that cause stress and consider how you might address that stress.

Devise self-care strategies:

Think about some activities that you can do that will help you feel better in each of these areas of your life.

Spending time with friends or developing Boundaries, for example, can be a way to build healthy social connections.

Plan for challenges:

When you discover you're neglecting a particular aspect of your life, create a change plan.

Take small steps:

You don't have to tackle everything all at once.

Identify one small step you can take to begin caring for yourself better.

Schedule time to focus on your needs:

Even when you feel like you don't have time to squeeze in one more thing, make self-care a priority. When you care for all aspects of yourself, you'll be able to operate more effectively and efficiently.

Identifying and Acknowledging Your Needs

What are my most important needs right now?

How do I feel when these needs are met?

How do I feel when they are not being met?

What actions can I take to fulfill these needs?

Self-Care
Check-In

What are you grateful for today?

What do you want to accomplish today?

Take 1 minute to breathe and re-center yourself.

What are your needs today?

How are you feeling today?

CREATE A SELF-CARE ROUTINE

Creating a self-care routine can be a powerful tool for promoting physical, emotional, and mental well-being. Here are some steps to help you create a self-care routine that works for you:

Identify your self-care needs:

Start by identifying activities or practices that make you feel relaxed, happy, and fulfilled. These may include exercise, spending time with loved ones, reading, or practicing meditation.

Prioritize self-care:

Commit to prioritize self-care in your daily routine.This may mean carving out time in your schedule for self-care activities. Set boundaries with others to protect your self-care time and making self-care a non-negotiable part of your routine.

Schedule self-care activities:

Schedule self-care activities into your calendar, just as you would schedule any other nBegin by incorporating small self-care practices into your daily routine. This may include taking a few minutes daily to meditate, walk, or practice deep breathing exercises. As you become more comfortable with these practices, you can gradually increase your time on self-care activities.

Experiment with different self-care practices:

Explore different self-care practices and find what works best for you. This may include trying new types of exercise, exploring new hobbies, or practicing different types of meditation or mindfulness techniques.

Be flexible:

Recognize that your self-care needs may change over time, and be flexible in adjusting your self-care routine accordingly. Allow yourself to explore new practices and activities, and be open to adapting your routine to meet your changing needs.

Remember, self-care is a journey, not a destination. Creating a self-care routine takes time and effort, but the benefits are well worth it.

By prioritizing self-care and creating a self-care routine, you can improve your overall well-being and live a happier, more fulfilling life.

Creating a *Self-Care* Plan

Moving Forward with Self-Care

Self-Care
Morning Routine

Starting your day with a self-care routine can set a positive tone for the rest of the day. Here are some steps to help you create a self-care morning routine:

Wake up at a consistent time:
Try to wake up at the same time each day, even on weekends, to establish a consistent sleep routine.

Hydrate:
Start your day by drinking a glass of water or a warm cup of tea to help hydrate your body and promote digestion.

Stretch or do some gentle movement:
Stretching or doing some gentle movement can help wake up your body and increase blood flow.

Practice mindfulness or meditation:
Take a few minutes to practice mindfulness or meditation to help calm your mind and reduce stress.

Have a healthy breakfast:
Eating a healthy breakfast can help you feel energized and focused for the day ahead.
Try to include foods that are rich in protein and complex carbohydrates.

Take a shower or bath:
Taking a shower or bath can help you feel refreshed and relaxed.
You can also add some essential oils or aromatherapy to enhance the experience.

Set intentions for the day:
Take a few minutes to set intentions for the day, such as focusing on self-care, practicing gratitude, or setting achievable goals.

Remember, everyone's self-care routine will be different, so it's important to find what works best for you. Try different practices and see how they make you feel, and don't be afraid to adjust your routine as needed. By starting your day with a self-care routine, you can set a positive tone for the rest of the day and improve your overall well-being.

Morning Affirmations

- I am grateful for the gift of a new day.

- I am rested, rejuvenated, and ready for a great day.

- This morning has so much potential and I am ready to harness it.

- I am excited about the opportunities today might bring.

- I will go about my day as the most confident version of myself.

- My body feels rested and I am ready to face the day.

- I invite love and joy into my life.

- I welcome all the gifts today might bring.

- Today I choose to cultivate habits that my future self will thank me for.

   I focus on what makes me feel good.

- I believe in myself.

- I am motivated and ready for the day ahead.

- I know I have what it takes to reach my goals.

- Today is a gift and I intend to make the most of it!

- I am driven to have a productive day.

- I am willing to work hard and be successful.

- This morning is the perfect opportunity to learn and grow. I am ready for an inspiring day.

What does your ideal
Morning Routine look like?

Self-Care Night Routine

Ending your day with a self-care routine can help you wind down, relax, and promote a better night's sleep.

Here are some steps to help you create a self-care night routine:

Set a bedtime:
Establish a consistent bedtime that allows for at least 7-8 hours of sleep per night.

Unplug from electronics:
Disconnect from electronic devices, such as your phone or computer, at least 30 minutes before bedtime to promote relaxation and reduce exposure to blue light.

Practice relaxation techniques:
Before bed, engage in relaxation techniques such as meditation, deep breathing, or gentle stretching to calm your mind and body.

Take a warm bath or shower:
Taking a warm bath or shower can help you relax and promote better sleep.

Engage in a soothing activity:
Engage in a soothing activity such as reading, journaling, or listening to calming music to help your mind unwind.

Use aromatherapy:
Use essential oils or aromatherapy to create a calming environment and promote relaxation. Lavender oil is known for its soothing properties and can be added to a diffuser or applied topically.

Practice gratitude:
Take a few minutes to reflect on the positive aspects of your day and practice gratitude.

Everyone's self-care routine will be different, so it's important to find what works best for you. Try different practices and see how they make you feel, and don't be afraid to adjust your routine as needed. Ending your day with a self-care routine can promote better sleep and improve your overall well-being.

Night Time Affirmations

I invite peace and serenity into my space.

I am calm, I am safe, I am at peace.

I honor my body and mind with rest so I can awaken as my best self.

I look forward to waking up well-rested and refreshed.

My body is held. This place is my sanctuary.

I am worthy of having a good night's sleep.

I release all that happened today and look forward to the adventures of tomorrow.

I have done enough today. It's time to rest.

I am relaxed and ready for sleep.

I forgive myself and others for any mistakes we made today.

I allow myself to rest easily.

I did my best today. Now I give myself the gift of sleep.

I invite my mind to be still.

I release all thoughts of worry and stress.

I call in nourishing and healing sleep.

Tomorrow is full of possibilities.

I allow myself to fall into a deep and restful sleep.

What does your ideal Night Time routine look like?

UNIT FOUR

PRACTICE SELF-COMPASSION

SOME THINGS TAKE TIME

Practicing self-compassion is an important aspect of self-care and can help improve your overall well-being. Here are some steps to help you practice self-compassion:

Acknowledge your emotions:
Take time to acknowledge and validate your emotions. Recognize that it's okay to feel a range of emotions and that you are not alone in experiencing them.

Speak kindly to yourself:
Practice speaking kindly to yourself and using positive self-talk. This can help counteract negative self-talk and boost your self-esteem.

Treat yourself with kindness:
Treat yourself with the same kindness and compassion you would offer to a loved one. This can involve taking care of your physical, emotional, and spiritual needs.

Practice mindfulness:
Practice mindfulness to help you stay present in the moment and avoid getting caught up in negative thoughts or worries.

Forgive yourself:
Forgive yourself for mistakes or shortcomings. Recognize that making mistakes is a normal part of being human and that you can learn and grow from them.

Self-compassion is not about being self-indulgent or making excuses for poor behavior.

Instead, it's about treating yourself with the same kindness and understanding you would offer to a good friend.

Practicing self-compassion can improve your overall well-being and build a healthier relationship with yourself.

Practicing Self-Compassion

What are some things you want to forgive yourself for?

List a few people you feel safe with:

How Would You Treat a Friend?

Perhaps the best way to provoke compassion is through this exercise: treating yourself like a good friend.

Giving our friends love, compassion, and understanding is easy, even when they fail or make a mistake. It can be much harder to extend that same understanding and compassion to ourselves when we make a mistake.

Follow these instructions to start showing yourself more compassion:

First, think about times when a close friend feels badly about them or struggles. How would you respond to your friend in this situation (especially when you're at your best)? Please write down what you typically do and say, and note how you usually talk to your friends.

Now, think about times when you feel bad about yourself or are struggling. How do you typically respond to yourself in these situations? Please write down what you usually do and what you say, and note the tone in which you talk to yourself.

Did you notice a difference? If so, ask yourself why. What factors or fears come into play that lead you to treat yourself and others so differently?

Please write down how you think things might change if you responded to yourself like you typically react to a close friend when you're suffering.

An exercise like this can be a first step toward treating yourself like a good friend – not just for a quick, 10-minute exercise, but for life.

Write a Letter of
Appreciation
to Yourself

UNIT FIVE

SET BOUNDARIES

Identifying Your Stressors

Stress Management

Establishing Self-Care Boundaries

Setting Reasonable Boundaries

Communicating Your Boundaries

Enforcing the Boundaries

UNIT SIX

GET
ENOUGH
REST

In a world that glorifies busyness and productivity, we must pause and recognize the significance of nurturing ourselves, both physically and mentally. We often neglect ourselves in our quest to achieve our goals and meet our responsibilities. We forget that we are not machines but human beings with limitations and vulnerabilities.

Self-care is about listening to your body and mind, acknowledging your needs, and tending to them with compassion. It means setting boundaries, saying 'no' when necessary, and permitting yourself to rest.

One critical aspect of self-care is getting enough rest. In a society that celebrates sleep deprivation as a badge of honor, we must remind ourselves that sleep is not a luxury but a biological necessity. During sleep, our bodies repair and rejuvenate, our memories are consolidated, and our minds find solace. When we deprive ourselves of sleep, we compromise our physical and mental health.

Chronic sleep deprivation has been linked to a host of health problems, including cardiovascular issues, weakened immune systems, and increased stress. It impairs our cognitive functions, making it difficult to concentrate, make decisions, and solve problems.

It can exacerbate mental health issues, such as anxiety and depression. It's not just about the quantity of sleep but also the quality. Restful sleep allows us to wake up refreshed, alert, and ready to face the day. Inadequate or restless sleep leaves us groggy, irritable, and less equipped to cope with life's challenges.

As we navigate our demanding lives, let us prioritize our physical and mental well-being, not as an indulgence but as a means to be our best selves.
Remember that you are worth the time and effort to care for yourself. Make self-care a daily practice, and prioritize rest as an essential part of your routine.

Tips to help you feel well rested:

Maintain a Consistent Sleep Schedule:

Try to go to bed and wake up at the same times every day, even on weekends. Consistency helps regulate your body's internal clock.

Create a Relaxing Bedtime Routine:

Establish a pre-sleep routine that helps you wind down. This might include activities like reading, taking a warm bath, or practicing relaxation techniques.

Optimize Your Sleep Environment:

Make sure your bedroom is dark, quiet, and at a comfortable temperature. Invest in a comfortable mattress and pillows that support your sleeping position.

Limit Exposure to Screens:

The blue light from screens (phones, tablets, TVs) can interfere with your sleep. Try to avoid screens at least an hour before bedtime.

Watch Your Diet:

Avoid heavy or spicy meals close to bedtime, as they can cause discomfort. Caffeine and nicotine are stimulants; avoid them in the hours leading up to sleep.

Limit Alcohol:

While alcohol may initially make you drowsy, it can disrupt your sleep cycle, causing you to wake up frequently during the night.

Exercise Regularly:

Regular physical activity can help you fall asleep faster and enjoy deeper sleep. However, avoid vigorous exercise too close to bedtime, as it can be stimulating.

Manage Stress and Anxiety:

To help calm your mind before bedtime, practice stress-reduction techniques, such as deep breathing, meditation, or progressive muscle relaxation.

Limit Naps:

While short power naps can be rejuvenating, long or irregular daytime naps can interfere with nighttime sleep. If you nap, keep it brief (20-30 minutes).

Be Mindful of What You Consume:

Drinking too many fluids before bedtime can result in nighttime awakenings to use the bathroom. Try to limit your fluid intake in the evening.

Get Plenty of Daylight:

Exposure to natural light during the day can help regulate your body's sleep-wake cycle. Spend time outdoors if possible.

Seek Professional Help:

If you've tried these tips and continue to have trouble sleeping or if you suspect a sleep disorder, it's essential to consult a healthcare professional.

Its Okay to *Rest*

UNIT SEVEN

CONNECT WITH OTHERS

Improved Relationships

In our modern world, we are constantly bombarded with demands and distractions. From work responsibilities to family obligations, we often give so much to others that we forget to nurture and care for ourselves. It's as if we're trying to fill the cups of others while our cups run empty.

But here's the truth: self-care is not selfish. It's not a luxury or a frivolous indulgence. It's fundamental for our physical, emotional, and mental well-being.

When we neglect self-care, we become depleted, stressed, and irritable, making it challenging to be our best selves in our relationships.

So, why is self-care essential for our relationships?

Resilience

Self-care builds resilience. When we take the time to recharge physically and mentally, we become better equipped to handle the inevitable challenges that life throws us. This means we're less likely to react impulsively in stressful situations, which can lead to conflicts in our relationships.

Self-care enhances our capacity for empathy. When well-rested and emotionally balanced, we are more attuned to the needs and feelings of others. We can listen more actively and respond compassionately, strengthening our bonds with our loved ones.

Setting Boundaries

Self-care empowers us to set healthy boundaries. By recognizing our own limits and needs, we can communicate them more effectively to those around us. This reduces resentment and burnout and fosters a culture of mutual respect in our relationships.

Lead by Example

Practicing self-care sets an example for others. When our loved ones see us prioritizing our well-being, they are more likely to do the same. Taking care of ourselves creates a ripple effect of positive habits within our families and social circles.

Quality Time

Self-care allows us to be fully present in our interactions. When not burdened by stress or exhaustion, we can enjoy quality time with our loved ones, making our connections deeper and more meaningful.

Personal Growth

Self-care supports our personal growth. When we invest in ourselves, we become better versions of ourselves. This growth can lead to more fulfilling relationships as we evolve and bring new perspectives and insights to our connections.

Self-care is an act of self-preservation and a gift to those we love. By caring for our physical, emotional, and mental well-being, we become better equipped to navigate the complexities of human relationships.

We become more compassionate, patient, and understanding individuals, capable of building stronger, more harmonious connections with others.
So, I encourage you to make self-care a priority in your life, not just for your sake but also for the sake of your relationships.

Remember, when you care for yourself, you're nurturing your happiness and creating the conditions for healthier, more fulfilling relationships with those you cherish most.

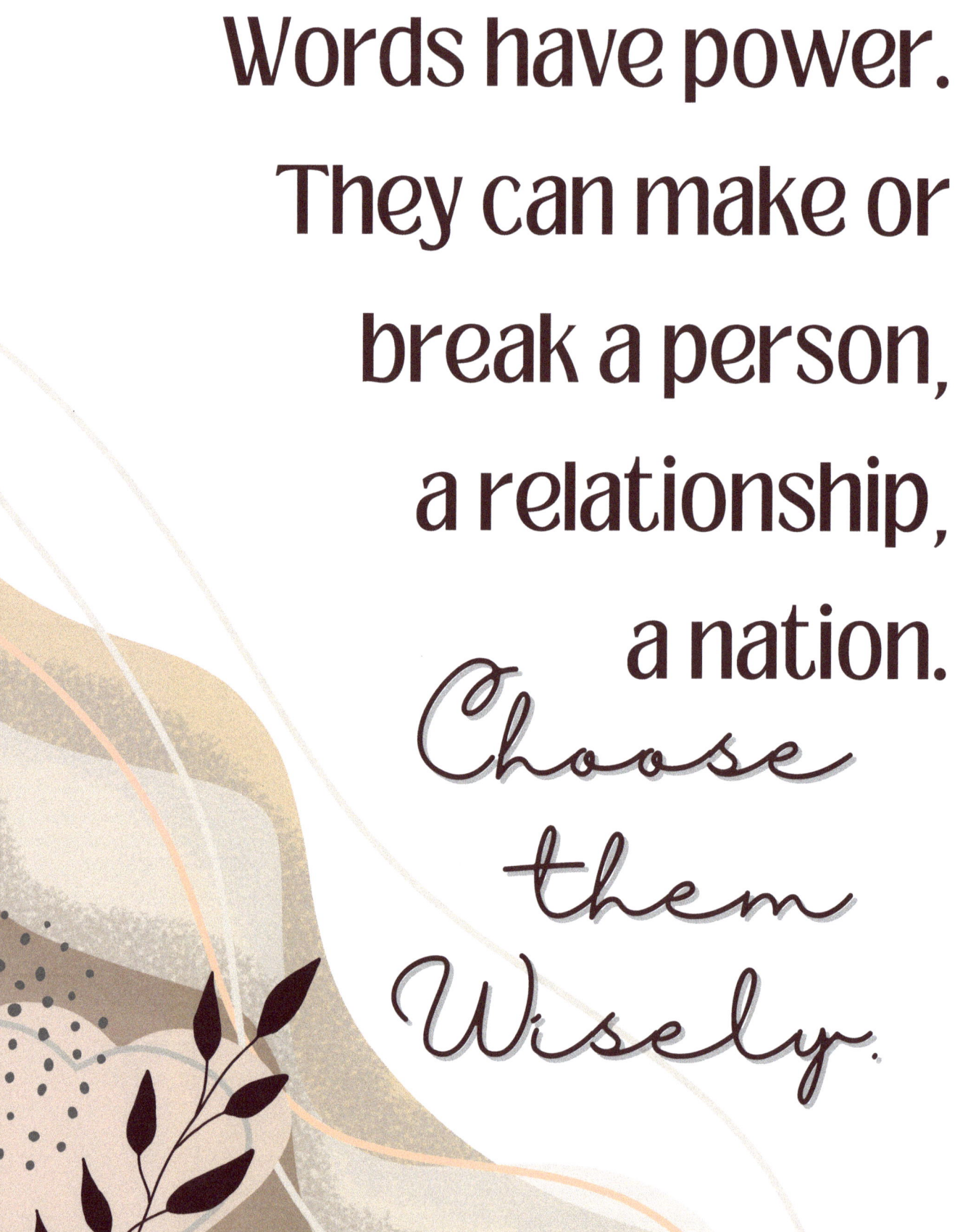

Words have power.
They can make or
break a person,
a relationship,
a nation.
Choose
them
Wisely.

UNIT EIGHT

TAKE CARE OF YOUR PHYSICAL HEALTH

Improved Physical Health

To understand self-care's importance in relation to physical health, we must first acknowledge what self-care entails.

Self-care encompasses a broad range of practices, from getting adequate rest, maintaining a balanced diet, engaging in regular physical activity, and managing stress to even taking time for relaxation and rejuvenation. These practices are not indulgences; they are the cornerstone of our health and vitality.

The link between self-care and physical health is undeniable. When prioritizing self-care, we embark on a journey to nurture our bodies, ensuring they function optimally. Adequate sleep, for instance, is essential for repairing and rejuvenating our cells, promoting cognitive function, and strengthening our immune system. Without it, our physical health deteriorates, making us susceptible to many ailments.

Likewise, a well-balanced diet provides our bodies with the essential nutrients for growth, repair, and overall health. Proper nutrition fuels our organs, muscles, and bones, enabling them to perform at their best.

Neglecting our dietary needs can lead to malnutrition, obesity, heart disease, and a range of other health issues. Exercise is yet another pillar of self-care with profound implications for physical health.

Regular physical activity improves our cardiovascular health and muscular strength and supports mental well-being by releasing endorphins, which alleviate stress and boost our mood.

Neglecting exercise can lead to a sedentary lifestyle, which is associated with a higher risk of chronic diseases, including diabetes and hypertension.

Self-care practices such as stress management and relaxation techniques directly impact our physical health.

Chronic stress can wreak havoc on our bodies, leading to inflammation, weakened immune response, and increased susceptibility to illnesses. By incorporating stress-reduction strategies into our daily lives, we can mitigate these harmful effects and fortify our physical resilience. It is also worth mentioning that self-care goes beyond the individual.

When we prioritize our own well-being, we set a positive example for those around us, inspiring them to do the same. Healthy individuals create healthier communities, which, in turn, positively impact society as a whole.

Self-care is not merely a matter of pampering oneself but of safeguarding one's physical health and longevity. By prioritizing self-care and adopting healthy practices in our daily lives, we enhance our physical well-being and increase our longevity, energy, and overall quality of life. Self-care is an investment in ourselves, and it pays dividends in terms of our health and happiness.

Remember that we have only one body, one vessel to carry us through life. Our responsibility is to care for, nurture, and cherish it.

I encourage you to make self-care a non-negotiable part of your daily routine. Embrace it not as a luxury but as a fundamental aspect of a long, healthy, and fulfilling life.

Why exercise?

Self-care is about improving ourselves, having more energy, and being more satisfied with the events happening in and around us.

Self-care involves a daily routine to achieve these goals by implementing the three core self-care methods, which, when used together, can lead to better well-being and happiness within oneself.

One of these core components of taking care of ourselves is exercise.

Regular exercise can improve our physical health, decrease our risk for severe health conditions, and help us feel better emotionally.

Benefits of Exercising

Self-care has several benefits, most of which are interlinked.

Committing to self-care should improve your well-being all around. Exercise can also be an excellent outlet for frustrations and anger (like martial arts or weight training).

It can take your mind off problems and troubling thoughts by placing you in a different environment and forcing you to focus on your deep breathing.

Understanding exercise's impact allows us to make intentional choices to improve our health.

Increased productivity

Now, let's talk about productivity.

It might seem counterintuitive that taking time for self-care could lead to increased productivity, but it's a proven fact. When well-rested, mentally clear, and emotionally stable, we are far more productive than when stressed, fatigued, or overwhelmed.

We can think more critically, solve problems more efficiently, and accurately complete tasks.

Self-care helps us avoid burnout, a common pitfall in today's fast-paced world. Burnout can lead to decreased productivity, absenteeism, and severe health issues.

By incorporating self-care into our daily routines, we create a protective buffer against burnout, ensuring that we can maintain high levels of productivity over the long term.
Self-care is a vital investment in our overall well-being and productivity. It empowers us to be the best versions of ourselves personally and professionally.

By practicing self-care, we become more resilient, focused, and capable of achieving our goals.

So, I implore you to make self-care a priority in your life.

Remember that taking care of yourself is not a luxury but an essential path to a more productive and fulfilling life.

Tips to Motivate and Maintain

Make it fun. It's essential to find ways to enjoy exercise and fit it into your lifestyle. Check out the athletics program and find one that really suits you.

Make a commitment. Schedule a time on your calendar or do anything else that can give you extra motivation to stick with it. It can also be helpful to set specific goals for yourself.

Mix it up

It's great to engage in a variety of activities so that you are working out different muscle groups. It also helps keep you interested and engaged.

Don't overdo it

Take it slowly, especially when you're starting, so you don't strain your muscles.

Every
Moment
is an opportunity
to change your
Perspective

JOURNALING
Prompts

What makes you feel powerful?

_____
_____
_____
_____
_____
_____
_____

What makes you feel in control?

_____
_____
_____
_____
_____
_____
_____
_____

What makes you feel like the best version of
YOU?
_____
_____
_____
_____
_____
_____
_____

Reflect on a time when you gave yourself permission to rest and recharge. How did you feel afterwards, and how can you prioritize rest in your life moving forward?

_____
_____
_____
_____
_____
_____
_____
_____

Reflect on a time when you felt truly passionate or inspired.

_____
_____
_____
_____
_____
_____
_____
_____

What are your core values, and how do they guide your daily life and decision-making?

_____
_____
_____
_____
_____
_____
_____
_____

What are some of your boundaries that you have with other people? Why are they important to you?

_____
_____
_____
_____
_____
_____
_____
_____

What type of self-care makes you feel guilty? Unpack why you think that might be and discover ways to give yourself compassion.

_____
_____
_____
_____
_____
_____
_____
_____
_____

What are your favorite hobbies? Why do you love them? What hobbies do you wish that you could start/get back into?

_____
_____
_____
_____
_____
_____
_____
_____

In what ways do you want to challenge yourself to step out of your comfort zone? It can include both small and big challenges.

_____
_____
_____
_____
_____
_____
_____

What is one way you can show yourself more empathy and leniency?

_____
_____
_____
_____
_____
_____
_____
_____
_____

What are your top five core values?

_____
_____
_____
_____
_____
_____
_____
_____

What is something that you're struggling with right now, and how can you show yourself kindness and compassion in this moment?

_____
_____
_____
_____
_____
_____
_____
_____

What is something you've been avoiding or putting off? What is holding you back? How can you take a small step towards addressing it today?

_____
_____
_____
_____
_____
_____
_____
_____

What do you wish other people knew about you?

_____
_____
_____
_____
_____
_____
_____

In what ways are you putting the needs of others before your own? What can you do to make sure you fill your own cup before tending to others?

_____

_____

_____

_____

_____

_____

_____

What qualities do you like about yourself that you value most?

_____

_____

_____

_____

_____

_____

_____

_____

What can you do to ground yourself more in the present moment

_____

_____

_____

_____

_____

_____

_____

_____

What is one small habit or routine that you can incorporate into your daily life to promote self-care and positivity?

_____

_____

_____

_____

_____

_____

_____

_____

Write down all of your self care goals for the next year, big or small.

_____

_____

_____

_____

_____

_____

_____

_____

_____

Write down all aspects of the perfect "you day".

_____

_____

_____

_____

_____

_____

_____

_____

What self care activities provide you with the most benefits?

_____

_____

_____

_____

_____

_____

_____

_____

What is something you've learned about your mental health that you've had a hard time coming to terms with?

_____

_____

_____

_____

_____

_____

_____

_____

Are you gentle to yourself on your "down" days? If not, how can you start showing yourself that gentleness?

_____

_____

_____

_____

_____

_____

_____

_____

What self care activity do you have an appreciation for now that you used to not? Why?

_____

_____

_____

_____

_____

_____

_____

When was the last time you felt burnt out and what led you to feel this way? What did you do to manage the burnout and what would you do in the future to prevent burnout?

_____

_____

_____

_____

_____

_____

_____

What is one positive affirmation you can focus on in your life?

_____

_____

_____

_____

_____

_____

_____

SEEKING SUPPORT

Seeking support when you're feeling overwhelmed or struggling with your mental or emotional well-being is essential.
There are many different ways to find help, including:

Talk to a loved one:
Sharing your feelings with a trusted friend or family can be a great way to find support. They can listen, offer advice, and be there for you when you need someone to talk to.

See a therapist:
A therapist can help you work through your emotions and challenges in a safe and supportive environment. You can find therapists in your area by searching online directories or through your insurance provider.

Join a support group:
Support groups are a great way to connect with others who are going through similar experiences. You can find support groups in your area by searching online or through local organizations.

Reach out to a helpline:
Many helplines available can provide support and resources if you're feeling overwhelmed or struggling with your mental health.

Remember, it's okay to ask for help when you need it. Seeking support is a sign of strength and can be essential in taking care of yourself.

This self-care workbook, which we've explored together, is a precious tool in this journey, a map to help us navigate the uncertain terrain of healing. It provides guidance, prompts us to reflect, and encourages us to prioritize self-compassion, self-love, and self-awareness. Through its pages, we've uncovered our resilience, tapped into our inner strength, and cultivated a deeper sense of self.

I hope this self-care workbook serves as a guiding light for your healing journey and a testament to the enduring strength that resides within each of us.

Through self-care, we can transcend the scars of our past and step into a brighter, more hopeful future.

May your journey toward healing be filled with self-compassion, self-discovery, and a renewed sense of purpose. In each day ahead, may you remember that you are worthy of love, happiness, and the life you dream of.

Embrace self-care as your ally, and let it be your constant companion on this transformative path. Thank you for your dedication to self-care and your healing journey. With resilience and self-compassion, you can overcome the wounds of the past and step into a future filled with hope and possibility.

with love,

Mckayla Julian